INCLINED PLANES

RAMP IT UP

SIMPLE MACHINES *FOR KIDS*

Andi Diehn

Illustrated by Micah Rauch

EXPLORE THE BIOMES IN THIS PICTURE BOOK SCIENCE SET!

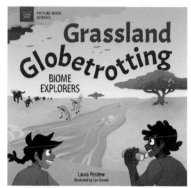

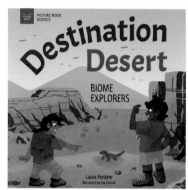

Check out more titles at www.nomadpress.net

Nomad Press

A division of Nomad Communications

10 9 8 7 6 5 4 3 2 1

This book was manufactured by CGB Printers,
North Mankato, Minnesota, United States
October 2023, Job #1066637

ISBN Softcover: 978-1-64741-102-2
ISBN Hardcover: 978-1-64741-099-5

Educational Consultant, Marla Conn

Questions regarding the ordering of this book should be addressed to
Nomad Press
PO Box 1036, Norwich, VT 05055
www.nomadpress.net

Printed in the United States.

Ramp it up! Science style.

Strap wheels on your feet and roll,

Thanks to a simple machine. (Or two!)

Heavy load? No problem!

Use a ramp to slide up, slide down,
whatever you need to move.

Dump it out! Turn a flat floor
into an inclined plane,

And watch the dirt crash
to the ground.

Science solves everything!

Imagine building a snowman.

The first snowball is *pretty easy*—you just roll it
to the size you want and let it rest on the ground.

The second snowball might be
a *little harder*—once it's big enough,
you need to lift it on top
of the first snowball.

And the third snowball?

That's a doozy!

What can you do
if your snowball is
TOO HEAVY
to lift onto the stack?

One thing
you can use is
A RAMP!

That **ramp** is a kind of simple machine—an **inclined plane!**

It's much LESS WORK to roll a heavy snowball up a slope than it is to lift it.

Simple machines help us do work.

An **inclined plane** is a *SLOPING* surface
that makes it easier to move **heavy things** *(such as snowballs)*
from <u>low ground</u> to <u>high ground.</u>

That heavy thing is called the **load.**

An inclined plane also makes it EASIER
to LOWER SOMETHING
by *sliding* it instead
of **dropping** it.

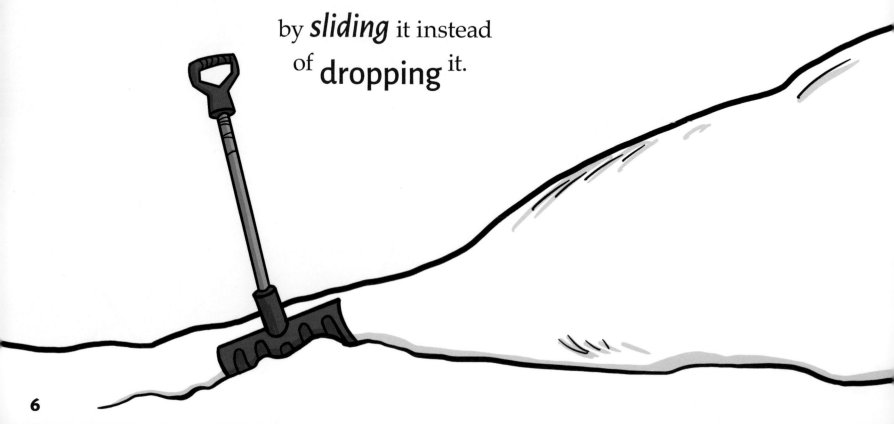

Imagine dropping that snowman's head on the ground—*splat!*

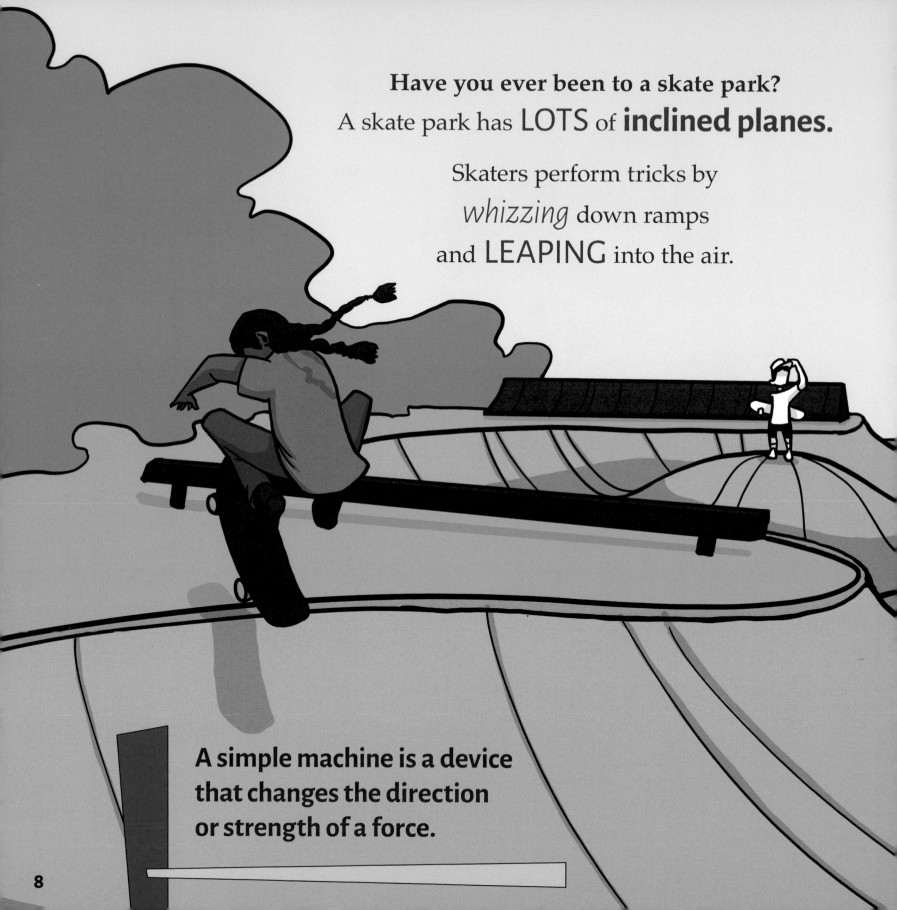

Have you ever been to a skate park?
A skate park has LOTS of **inclined planes**.

Skaters perform tricks by
whizzing down ramps
and LEAPING into the air.

**A simple machine is a device
that changes the direction
or strength of a force.**

8

On their way down, skaters land back
on the ramp and *coast*.

Where else do you see ramps?

Other simple machines include screws, levers, wedges, pulleys, and wheels and axles.

You might see a ramp in front of the **library** or your **school.**

People who have **a lot to carry** or who use a **wheelchair** find it EASIER to take the **ramp.**

Inclined planes aren't always smooth and **FLAT.**

Stairs are another example of an **inclined plane!**

Imagine climbing a ladder that's STRAIGHT UP and down to get to the upper levels of your house.

That's going to take a lot of energy.

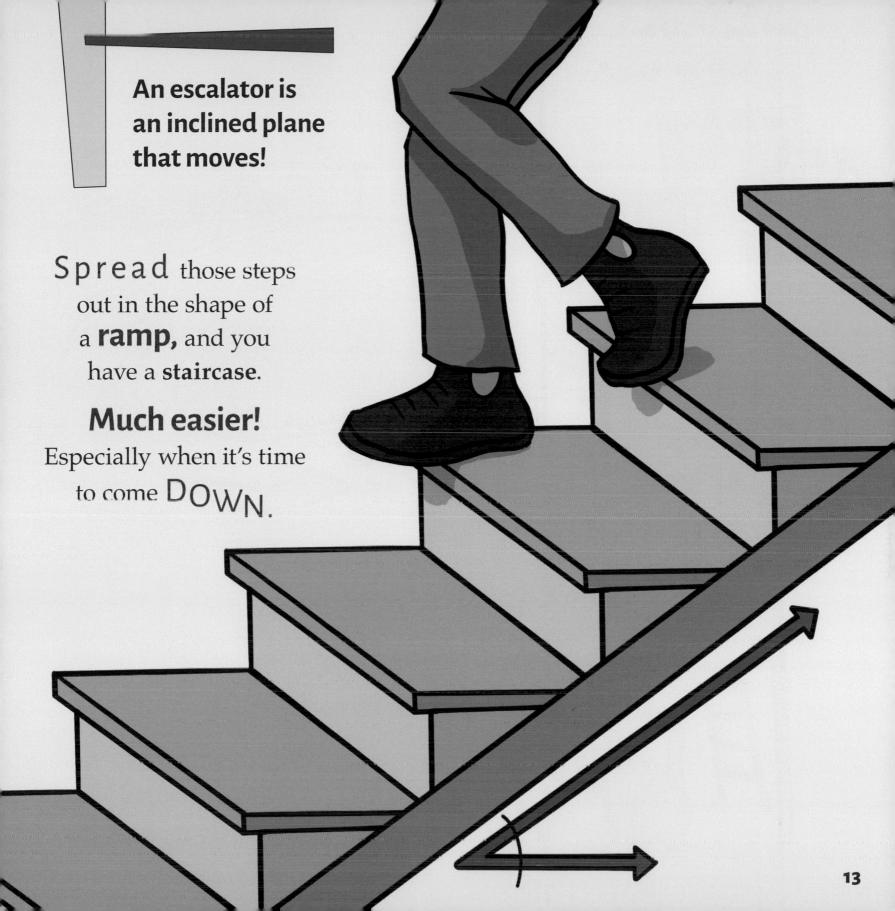

An escalator is an inclined plane that moves!

Spread those steps out in the shape of a **ramp,** and you have a **staircase.**

Much easier! Especially when it's time to come DOWN.

Some inclined planes are **fixed in place.**

Think of a ramp that cars DRIVE UP to get to the highway or the slide you *whizz down* at the playground.

Other inclined planes have to be **activated.**

Have you ever watched a dump truck dump its load?
The driver raises the back of the truck to form an
inclined plane and all the stuff *slides out!*
The back goes from **FLAT** to **SLOPED**
to do its work as a ramp.

Remember, simple machines make it easier for us to do work. **How?**

By giving us something called a **mechanical advantage.**

A mechanical advantage makes your pushing and pulling forces much more powerful than when you use only your own muscles.

An inclined plane gives you a mechanical advantage that makes *pushing* a load **UP A RAMP** take a lot less energy than **LIFTING** it.

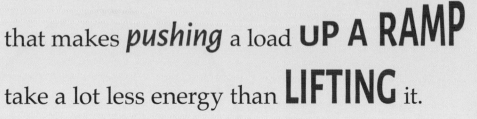

But it's not always easy.

Friction makes it more difficult to move a load.

Friction is a **force** that **slows down** objects when they rub against each other.

When you push a heavy box **UP A RAMP,** the **friction** between the box and the ramp **slows** you down.

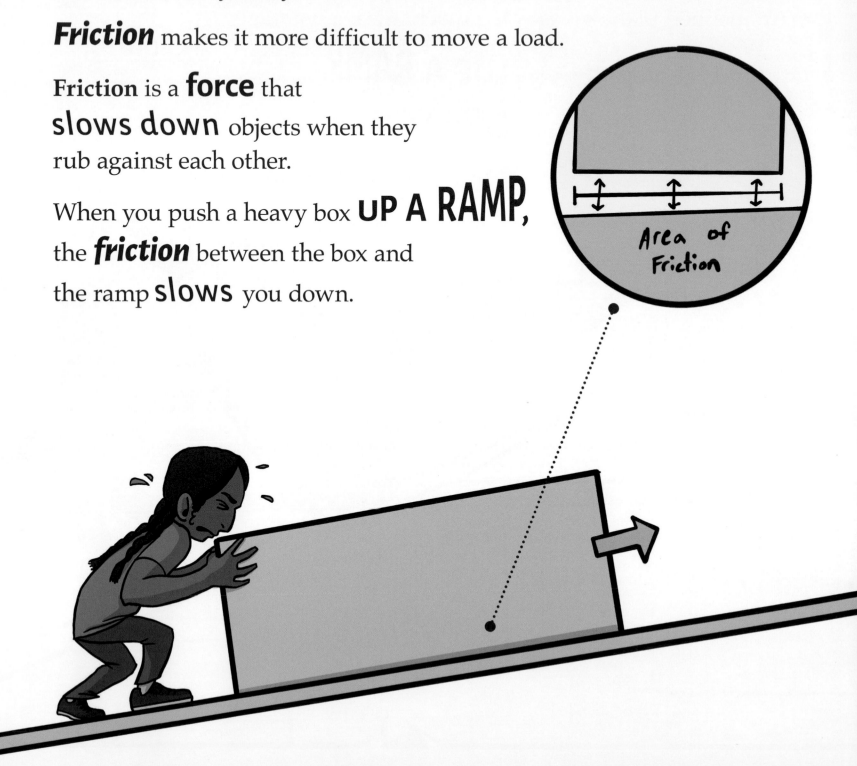

Area of Friction

Put that box on **wheels** and most of the *friction* goes away!

When you use a ramp to ease a **HEAVY** object to the **ground,**
friction is going to slooooooow
down that heavy thing.

That can be a good thing!

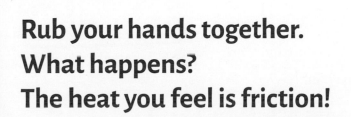

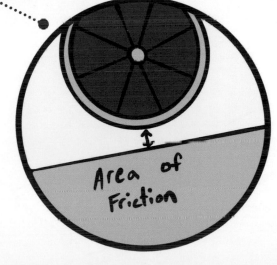

Area of Friction

Rub your hands together.
What happens?
The heat you feel is friction!

Inclined planes are very useful and easy to make.

Early humans probably used them to
move heavy objects,
just as we do today.

Ancient Romans built *SLOPING AQUEDUCTS* so water could flow from its source to people in towns and cities.

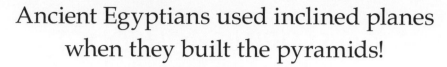

Ancient Egyptians used inclined planes
when they built the pyramids!

They *moved* ENORMOUS BLOCKS
of stone over ramps to form those
HUGE monuments.

Have you heard of Stonehenge?

Stonehenge is a ring of
ENORMOUS STONE COLUMNS
that stand in a field in England.

Historians think that about **4,500 years ago,** ancient humans used **ramps** made from dirt to settle these **MASSIVE STONES.**

Do we know this for sure? No! Dirt ramps don't last over time.

But we can **wonder!**

You can find **inclined planes** all around your neighborhood!

Look and make a list!

A water slide

A ramp on a moving van

A funnel

A slanted roof

Make a Marble Run!

What You Need

*cardboard tubes - tape -
books or blocks - marbles*

What You Do

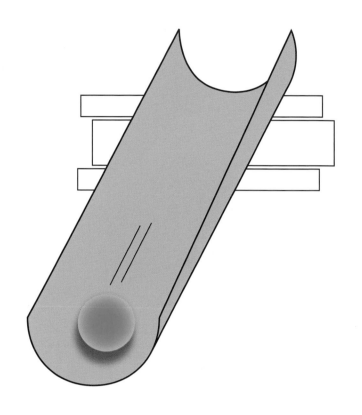

- Ask an adult to cut the cardboard tubes the long way so you can see inside. These are your inclined planes!

- Tape the pieces of tubes together to make longer and shorter runs.

- Stack books or blocks and balance your runs across these, making a pattern for the marbles to roll down.

Try It Out! Put a marble at a high end and watch it make its way down. Do you need to move your runs for the marble to roll all the way to the end?

Glossary

aqueduct: a channel for moving water.

force: a push or pull that changes an object's motion.

friction: a force that slows objects when they rub against each other.

inclined plane: a sloped surface that connects a lower level to a higher level.

lever: a bar that rests on a support and lifts or moves things.

load: an applied force or weight.

mechanical advantage: the amount a machine increases or changes a force to make a task easier.

pulley: a wheel with a grooved rim that a rope or chain is pulled through to help lift a load.

ramp: a sloping surface.

screw: an inclined plane wrapped around a central axis used to lift objects or hold things together.

simple machine: a device that changes the direction or strength of a force. The six simple machines are the inclined plane, lever, pulley, screw, wedge, and wheel and axle.

slope: a surface that has one end or side at a higher level than the other.

wedge: thick at one end and narrow at the other, a wedge is used for splitting, tightening, and securing objects.

wheel and axle: a wheel with a rod that turn together to lift and move loads.

work: the force applied to an object to move it across a distance.

Inclined Plane

Wedge

Lever

SIMPLE MACHINES

Pulley

Screw

Wheel and Axle